Imre Kiralfy's Columbus and the Discovery of America ..

A Most Noble Theme Profusely Illustrated with Living Tableaux.

EMBELLISHED WITH GRAND SCENES, REALISTIC BATTLES,
SHIPS IN MOTION, TREMENDOUS PAGEANTS AND
EXQUISITE PICTURESQUE BALLETS.

IMRE KIRALFY'S

COLUMBUS

AND THE

Discovery of America.

THE GRANDEST AND MOST COLOSSAL SPECTACLE OF ALL TIME.

DEPICTING WITH HISTORICAL TRUTH AND ACCURACY THE LIFE,
TRIALS, DISCOVERIES AND TRIUMPHS OF

CHRISTOPHER COLUMBUS,

AND ADAPTED AND ARRANGED FOR PRODUCTION WITH

BARNUM & BAILEY'S

GREATEST SHOW ON EARTH,

ON THE LARGEST STAGE EVER CONSTRUCTED.

INCIDENTALLY INTRODUCING THE CHIEF HISTORICAL EVENTS CONTEMPORANEOUS WITH THE

FIRST VOYAGE TO THE NEW WORLD.

THE COURIER COMPANY, SHOW PRINTERS, BUFFALO, N. Y.

The Boulevard Velvet

"FAN" VELOUETTE

AND

Velouette "Sans Rival"

This make claims
Superiority
over all others

Sold by all the leading Dry Goods and Millinery Houses throughout the United States.

The most Popular Brands of Velvets suitable for Dress and Millinery purposes.

The latest
improvement in
PILE FABRICS

The Most Popular
—Brands of— VELVETS
Sold by all the Leading
DRY GOODS & MILLINERY HOUSES

THANKS TO MR. KIRALFY.

We desire, in the most public and unreserved manner, to express our congratulations to Mr. Imre Kiralfy upon the magnificent triumph he has achieved in producing his latest spectacle, which is undoubtedly his masterpiece, "Columbus and the Discovery of America," and to thank him for the extraordinary display of energy and industry which has well deserved and splendidly won for him his great success, and which has satisfactorily inured to our mutual advantage. To perfect this part of our exhibition required the highest order of artistic creation, adaptation and invention, and he has far surpassed our most sanguine expectations in these respects and more than justified our confidence in his ability and experience. While unlimited means have been placed at his disposal, he has utilized them with rare judgment and effect, and the result is a most splendid and impressive series of classic displays and tableaux, which we are confident all America will join in pronouncing altogether unparalleled.

BARNUM & BAILEY.

A WORD FROM THE AUTHOR.

In my composition of this vivid pictorial illustration of the various epochs in the life and career of the immortal discoverer of the New World, I have been animated by the rareness of the opportunity to supply a fitting representation of this most heroic theme, and as each recurring Columbus celebration occurs only once in a century, and being fortunate enough to have this anniversary of the fourth centennial of the discovery of America come within the period of my life, and wishing to do homage to the great and immortal navigator on this occasion, I have striven earnestly to make this historical production the greatest of all my works.

In this gigantic undertaking *all my studies, experience* and energy have been devoted to placing before the public not a mere series of tableaux, but to supply a faithful, authentic, and complete reproduction of the chief historic incidents in the life of that great mariner, in the order in which they occurred.

In presenting to the American public the latest and grandest original historical spectacle of "Columbus and the Discovery of America," I wish to most earnestly assure them that it will be even more magnificent than the great one of last year.

I have endeavored to perfect an entirely original historical spectacle in novel shape and combined panoramic and dioramic form; an enterprise requiring a colossal stage, far beyond the space at command of any building in America. The huge amphitheatrical tent expressly devised and constructed by Messrs. Barnum and Bailey for that purpose, affords the only opportunity for the successful presentation of a series of realistic tableaux and processions far grander than anything of the kind heretofore attempted, and for the display and utilization of scenic effects, which of necessity must be proportionately colossal. Of this I have conscientiously sought to take fullest advantage, both in immensity of production, treatment of the enormous surface of canvas employed, artistic correctness and harmony in association and coloring of scenery and costumes, and both aggregation and individuality of effects.

Finally, I desire to express my most greatful appreciation of the unbounded liberality and confidence accorded me by Messrs. Barnum and Bailey in the prosecution and perfection of this great work.

This production is an inspiration evoked by the splendor of its theme, and is offered as my humble tribute to the greatest genius of the centuries, Christopher Columbus.

NEW YORK, March, 1892.

IMRE KIRALFY.

IMRE KIRALFY'S
CHRISTOPHER COLUMBUS

Superb Music expressly composed by
Signor ANGELO VENANZI.

The Italian Poetry and Words of Songs by
Signor ANGELO BIGNOTTI.

The entire Historical Costumes and Accessories designed by
Signor ALFRED EDEL.
Executed by Monsieur EDMOND LANDOLFF.

Costumes of the Oriental Ballet in the Alhambra Scene expressly designed by
WILHELM.
Executed by Miss FISHER.

Magnificent Scenery designed and executed by
Messieurs AMABLE and GARDY.

Chorus and Music under the Direction of
Signor BENIAMINO LOMBARDI.

Stage and Choreographic Director,
Signor ETTORE COPPINI.

Entire Spectacle produced, conceived, designed, organized and produced by
IMRE KIRALFY,
The Author of "Nero," "Venice in London," etc., etc.

CAST OF CHARACTERS.

———————•———————

CHRISTOPHER COLUMBUS, The Discoverer
FERDINAND, King of Castile and Arragon
ISABELLA, Queen of Castile and Arragon
PRINCESS ISABELLA, their Daughter

DONNA BEATRIX DE BOBADILLA, Marchioness de Moya.
BOABDIL EL CHICO, King of Granada.
MUZA BEN ABEL GAZAN, Moorish Chief
ABUL CAZIN ABDEL MELU, Governor of the City of Granada

CIDI YAHYE, Cousin to El Zegal, and afterward Don Pedro de Granada
THE SANTON HAMET ABEN ZARRAX
AYXA LA HARRA, Mother of Boabdil
ZARAMA, Wife of Boabdil
ABEN COMIXA, the Vizier.
THE MARQUIS OF CADIZ
DON ALONZO DE AGUILLAR
HERNANDO PEREZ DE PULGAR

FRIAR ANTONIO MILLAN, Prior of the San Franciscan Convent in the Holy City
RODRIGO DE MENDEZ, Son of the Grand Cardinal
LOUIS FERNANDO PUERTO CARERO.
MARTIN CALINDO.

MOHAMMED BEN HASSAN, the aged Alcayde of Baza.
ALI BEN FAHAR, the true and faithful Moorish Warrior.
MULEY ABDALLAH.
MARTIN ALONZO PINZON.

Spanish Cavaliers and Knights, Moorish Warriors, Nobles, Pages, Crusaders, Hid-
algoes, Clergymen, Courtiers, Peasants, Sailors, Pilots, Indians, Chiefs, Mariners,
Viziers, Priests, Notaries, Magistrates, Christian Captives, Moorish Prisoners,
Ecclesiastics, Servants, Slaves, Princes, Soldiers, Male and Female
Chorus Singers, Dancing Girls, Troubadours, Muleteers, Artisans,
Shipwrights, Armorers, Body Guards, Heralds, etc., etc.

GENERAL SYNOPSIS OF SCENES.

SCENE I.

The Alhambra Palace.

King Boabdil and his Favorites
Female Chorus in the Moonlight
Moorish Dancing Girls and Music

The Starving People Seeking the King.
The King Promises a Feast
Sublime and Picturesque Ballet

Preparations within the City for Battle
The Warriors Chant War Songs
Departure for the Battle Field

Mounting the Battlements to Witness the Fight
Female Chorus of Songs for Victory
Return of the Defeated Moors to the City

Flight of the Women for Safety
Demanding the City's Surrender
King Boabdil El Chico Holds a Council of War
Agreeing to Surrender.
Departure of the Moors from Granada

Triumphal Occupation of the City by the Spaniards.
The Flag of Castile Floats from the Alhambra
Ferdinand and Isabella Leading the Army

Grand Victory Procession.

Closing of the Gates against the Moors
Triumph of the Cross over the Crescent
Columbus Again Urging his Scheme

Queen Isabella agrees to Pledge her Jewels for the Voyage
Liberation of Christian Captives.
Chanting the Te Deum for Victory

Grand Chorus.

GENERAL SYNOPSIS OF SCENES.

(*CONTINUED.*)

———•———

SCENE II.

The Ancient Port of Palos, August 3, 1492.

Columbus Preparing for his Voyage.

Reading the King's Proclamation.

Martin Alonzo Pinzon appears.

Receiving the Blessing of the Priests.

Hoisting the Flag on the Santa Maria.

Embarking on the Caravels.

Farewells to Columbus and his Followers.

Grand Chorus of Farewell.

Departure of the Ships.

SCENE III.

The First Voyage of Discovery.

Becalmed on the Ocean.

Columbus Notices the Needle's Variation.

A Storm at Sea.

Floating Trees and Driftwood Discovered.

Discontent of the Crew.

Quelling the Mutiny on the Santa Maria.

Martin Pinzon Mistakes a Cloud for Land.

Columbus Discovers the Moving Light on Shore.

The Pinto Discharges a Gun.

Columbus and the Crews Sing Chorus of Thanks.

Land at last Discovered.

SCENE IV.

The First Landing in the New World.

Fright and Terror of the Indians.

Columbus Approaches in his Boat.

Taking Formal Possession.

THE STORY OF

COLUMBUS ──AND THE── DISCOVERY OF AMERICA.

As Portrayed in the Dramatic Action of the Nautical, Martial, Musical, Poetical, Terpsichorean, Processional and Pantomimical Spectacle in the

BARNUM & BAILEY GREATEST SHOW ON EARTH,

AS ARRANGED AND DESIGNED BY

IMRE KIRALFY.

SCENE I.

Un,

.ourt of the Alhambra Palace—Night of January 1, 1492.

CHARACTERS IN THIS SCENE.

Γ

Christopher Columbus
Ferdinand, King of Castile and Arragon.
Ysabella, Queen of Castile and Arragon
Cavalier Tendilla.
Alonzo de Quintanilla (afterwards Archbishop of Granada).
Friar Juan Perez (formerly Confessor to the Queen).
Boabdil El Chico, King of Granada.
Aben Comixa, the Vizier.
Abdul Cazin Abdul Melu, Governor of the City of Granada
Muza Ben Abdul Gazin, Moorish Chief.
The Santon Hamet Aben Zarrax
Adi Yalige (now known as Dom Pedro de Granada)
Ayxa la Horra, Mother of Boabdil
Zorayma, his Wife
The Son of the Moorish King (a child)
Spanish Hidalgoes, Nobles, Clergy, Soldiery, Courtiers, Pages, Moorish Knights and People of both sexes

This poetic scene represents the courtyard within the fortress of the Alhambra   Alhambra, meaning "red castle," is a name given to the fortress which formed a sort of acropolis or citadel to the City of Granada, and in which stood the palace of the ancient Moorish kings. It was built about six hundred years ago, in the year 1238, and a part of it still remains to-day. A view of the palace is shown in this scene as it existed four hundred years ago, with its huge massive gates and grand approaches to the city, which the castle itself guarded from invading foes. Beyond this the view embraces glimpses of the landscape, with the Spanish encampment in the City of Santa Fé.

Our tableau opens with King Boabdil El Chico, surrounded by his wives, favorites and slaves. The time is midnight. Presently music greets the ear, the female slaves begin the slow, sensuous movements of oriental dances, while songs by female slaves are heard accompanied by the wild, wierd, mysterious music of quaint instruments, and the scene gradually becomes one of splendor.

MOORS PREPARING TO MEET THE SPANIARDS BEFORE GRANADA

SONGS OF FEMALE SLAVES.

Quando alla sera spuntano
Neo ciel gli astri d'or.
Innamorati e teneri
Cantan gli augelli ancor.
E dicon:—Bruna Almea
Fanciulla bruna;
Vedi la nivea Dea
Avvolge un vel.
Noi ineggian la luna
Ed alle stelle,
Che innamorate e belle
Stan nel ciel.

Quando al mattino pallidi
Muojono gli astri d'or
Qui in terra astri piu vividi
Brillan nel giorno ancor.
Le tue pupille o Almea
Piu delle stelle
Sun scintillanti e belle
E han piu fulgor.
Or posa come Dea
Sul serto aurato,
Viva per te beato
Il tuo signor.

When shades of evening gently fall,
And golden stars appear.
"Good-night, the birds so sweetly call,
Telling of love so dear.
And soon the silvery moonbeams show,
As through a veil, the plains below.
In beauty shines the moon
With stars around,
And love and beauty seem
Here to abound.
Our song would tell you where
They may be found.

But ah! when in the morning gray
The golden stars do die,
Thy brilliant eyes, Almea, say
'Stars are not in the sky.
For morning light doth make stars dim,
They fade when birds begin their hymn.
Thine eyes are still more bright,
More beauties show,
Brighter than stars at night,
More lustrous glow,
And ever in thy sight
True love will grow.

Suddenly, low murmurings are heard without, which gradually coming nearer and nearer, the scene is rudely broken by the entrance of the Santon Hamet Aben Zarrax, followed by a riotous mob of starving people. Santon Hamet demands of the king food for the citizens, which they have been unable to get owing to the circumvallation of the city by the Spaniards.

King Boabdil, to appease them, promises them a battle on the morrow, at which the rage of the people is turned to rejoicing and praise for the king. The latter, to further divert the minds of the mob, orders a grand festival to be prepared at once, which the populace shall be permitted to see, and directs that they shall be served with wines and fruits, upon hearing which announcement the people become almost wild with pleasure.

ENTRANCING MOORISH DANCES.

Moorish maidens now replace the scenes of discontent with a romantic and picturesque series of entrancing dances, while the people are feasted with the remaining stores. The festival is interrupted by the appearance of armed citizens, and the warriors are marshalled by Muza, their idolized leader, who inspires the troops with hopes of victory.

Songs of joy are chanted, the priests bestow their blessings on the warriors, the people sing choruses, in which they are joined by the troops, and with the songs still ringing in their ears the army, led by Muza and King Boabdil, depart from the city to the plains to offer battle to the Spaniards.

While the warriors are sallying forth, the old and crippled, with the women and children remain behind. At the first sounds of the conflict some mount the battlements to obtain a view of the impending struggle, while others chant prayers for victory.

COLUMBUS AT THE SURRENDER OF GRANADA

CHORUS OF PRAYER.

Oh, sommo Alà potente	Allah, in thy might and power,
Nostro Signor clemente,	Help us in this awful hour.
Abbi di noi pietà	Allah, hear our suppliant cry,
Sommo potente Alà.	Rising to thy throne on high.

While the sounds of song of female voices are dying away small detachments of soldiers come flying into the city, and the news is quickly told of the total defeat of the Moors.

A scene of wild confusion follows quick and fast. Mothers fly in terror to hide their children, others again rush to secure and secrete their valuables, while everybody seems bent upon gaining a place of safety and security from the approaching victorious Spaniards.

Muza and King Boabdil now re-enter in despair and disconsolately await the inevitable summons to surrender.

An envoy from the victorious Ferdinand appears demanding the unconditional surrender of the palace and town, which terms King Boabdil and his adviser, Abdul Cazin, are compelled to accept.

Capitulation being decided upon, the envoy departs, taking with him a number of hostages, among whom is the son of Boabdil.

Preparations are now begun for the evacuation, and Axya la Horra, the mother of Boabdil, and Zorayma, his wife, with some of his favorites, together with his entire household and a few faithful warriors, take their departure and bid a last farewell to Granada. Meanwhile Boabdil and Cazin meet the approaching Ferdinand and Isabella, and while attempting to kneel before them, they are restrained by the king, who magnanimously raises and embraces Boabdil and restores to him the son who has been held as a hostage.

The Moorish king then delivers the keys of the city to Ferdinand, who hands them to Queen Isabella.

·QUEEN ISABELLA OFFERING HER JEWELS·

These ceremonies over, King Boabdil takes a last look at the palaces which for so many years have been the residence of the Moorish kings, and departs forever from that place.

The victorious Spaniards (having entered and taken possession of the captured city, the last in the hands of the Moors, the conquest of which

COPYRIGHTED BY IMRE KIRALFY 1891

closed for all time the series of wars extending over centuries, and resulting in the entire Moorish domains in Spain coming under the authority of Castile and Arragon) now enter the Alhambra   The flags of Castile and Arragon are hoisted over the towers, while the army, with Ferdinand and Isabella at the head, accompanied by the Cavalier Tendilla, Alonzo de Quintannella and the chivalry of Spain, together with Columbus, the Friar Juan Perez, and others, enter its gates amid salvos of artillery and the grand ceremonies attendant upon it.

Columbus again urges the king to consider his project, and it is at this moment that the queen, with a sudden burst of inspired enthusiasm, declares in the words which have become historical .   "I will undertake the enterprise for my own crown of Castile, and will pledge my jewels if . the funds in the treasury are found inadequate."

Columbus, almost overcome by this great turn in the tide of his fortunes, is inspired by gratitude and joins with enthusiasm in the songs of praise which express the general joy that the long wars have ended.

SONG OF VICTORY

Sta gloria eterna a Dio
Che ci difese ancora ;
E or salga ardente e pio
L'inno di gloria al ciel

Now God above we humbly praise,
  He fighteth ever by our side
Sweet songs of thanks to Heaven we raise,
  Our Lord doth us to vict'ry guide

THE TRIUMPHAL ENTRY OF COLUMBUS INTO BARCELONA, UPON HIS RETURN FROM THE DISCOVERY OF AMERICA.

SCENE II.

The Ancient Port of Palos, August 3, 1492.

CHARACTERS IN THIS SCENE

Christopher Columbus.

Martin Alonzo Pinzon,
Francisco Martin Pinzon, } Brothers
Vicente Yanez Pinzon

Friar Juan Perez

Sancho Ruiz,
Pedro Alonzo Nino, } Pilots
Bartholomeo Roldan.

Rodrigo Sanchez, Inspector General

Diego de Arana, Chief Alguazil

Rodrigo de Escobedo, a Royal Notary

A Physician

A Surgeon

Adventurers, Servants, Mariners, People, Soldiers

A Magistrate.

A Notary of Palos.

After Queen Isabella has agreed to supply the necessary funds for the equipment of the vessels which were to carry Columbus and his daring followers on their perilous voyage, no time was lost in making all the needed preparations.

The present view opens at the little port of Palos in Spain. In the river, close by, are seen the "Pinta," "Nina," and "Santa Maria," the latter the caravel which Columbus himself is to command. The shore seems alive with bustle and excitement, for at no time in the history of the little port was there ever so important an event. Convoys of soldiers and the people are canvassing the probable result of the voyage and speculating upon the chances of its ever returning. The magistrate mounts the steps leading to the church, followed by soldiers, while an official reads the king's proclamation.

O popolo di Spagna, pel Sovrano	Draw near, ye loyal men of Spain, and give attention
Voler del nostro Re,	Unto the words I say—
Proclama a chi fu di partir eletto	By order of the King It is his pleasure,
Che se all' appello regal mancar dovesse	That all, who for this voyage were selected,
Dal sacro tribunale condannato	Proceed to work, and give up ease and leisure
Verra, senza perdon, all' Auto-da-fé.	That all obey at once it is expected
Vi sovvenga il voler del nostro Re	In case of non-compliance the sharp measure
	Of death will be the doom of those detected

Martin Alonzo Pinzon, with his two brothers, who are to command the "Pinta" and "Nina," now prepare to embark on their respective ships

Columbus appears shortly after with Rodrigo Sanchez of Segovia, the inspector general, Diego de Arana, Chief Alguazil and Rodrigo Escobedo, the royal notary, followed by the physician and surgeon and a band of adventurers.

THE·DEPARTURE·OF·COLUMBUS·FROM·THE·PORT·OF·PALOS·ON·THE·3ᵈ·OF·AUGUST·1492·

After receiving a blessing from Friar Juan Perez, and other appropriate religious ceremonies having taken place, the intrepid body of navigators proceed to embark for their vessels.

The shores are now thronged with people and the place appears as on a holiday. The women of Palos approach Columbus and wish him God-speed.

BACCHAROLE.

A te la sorte—or sia propizia	Oh, warrior bold! oh, chief of faith supreme!
Guerrier in vitto—	May fortune's smiles benign on thee attend,
Dona la speme—nuova letizia,	Thy safe return is more than a mere dream,
E il tuo ritorno—ci allieti il cor.	Such fervent hope to us new life doth lend.
Ora fidente—nel tuo destino	Thy destiny for thee marks out the way
Tu novi ardito—nella tua fé.	May all thy paths be ever soft with flowers,
Noi spargiam fiori—sul tuo cammino	And, great in faith, thy feet shall never stray
Ed invochiamo— il ciel per te.	While for thine aid we call on heaven's powers.

Columbus, after receiving the benediction of his friend Friar Juan Perez, and amid the vocal peans of those assembled, starts upon his grand voyage across unknown and unexplored waters to enrich civilization with a new world and its boundless treasures.

The whole assembled community break out into a grand chorus of farewell, which is added to by the pealing of the bells in the churches, and as the majestic flood of music and song floats upon the air, the boats are seen to row off.

CHORUS OF FAREWELL

Il gran nocchiero nel destin fidente
Cerca la nuova terra e nuova vita,
Sia fido il vento a il ciel gli sia clemente
Possa immortal fortuna su quel crine
Posar l'alloro ; e la sognata e ambita
Gloria alla terra e al mar senza confine
Ridir le gesta e il suo valor cantar

To search for shores unknown, new forms of life,
  Columbus boldly goes, trusting to fate
May wind and sea alike be free from strife,
  May Neptune never shake his trident dread
Upon those brows immortal fame will place
  A laurel crown, and honors on him wait
Thus all the earth and sea his deeds may trace,
  And know the path the great explorer led

Coro di Marinai.

O nostra terra, O Spagna
Ci rivedremo ancor ;
La speme ci accompagna,
Ci sara guida ognor
O nostra patria , O Spagna
Con te rimane il cor.

Chorus of Sailors on the Boats

Oh Spain ! beloved land, farewell !
  Farewell for many years,
A constant faith with us doth dwell,
  Henceforth we have no fears
Eternal hope will sweetly tell—
  Dry, dry, those idle tears

Coro, sulla piazza.

Addio compagni , O figli nostri addio,
Le nostri preci il cielo ascolterà
Voi pur nell' ansia e nel terror Iddio
Sempre invocate e Lui v'assisterà

Chorus on the Shore

Farewell ! farewell ! our sons and comrades dear,
  To heaven above our prayers will daily rise.
Remember ever, God is always near,
  And lends attentive ears to plaintive cries

SCENE III.

The First Voyage to the New World.

After leaving the Port of Palos the vessels are represented as encountering a calm at sea. The sails flap against the masts and the three caravels are apparently motionless. At early sunrise, a breeze springing up, the fleet is gently wafted on its way.

Columbus, while intently watching the compass, is amazed to discover that the needle has varied, and calls the attention of the pilot to the strange and remarkable occurrence, cautioning him not to divulge the matter to the crew for fear of its alarming them.

A storm arising, the vessels roll and pitch, and at its subsidence a brilliant meteor is seen falling from the heavens, causing the sailors much fear. Birds of various kinds are now noticed flying about the ships which, together with many kinds of driftwood and floating bushes, are taken as sure indications of the approach to land, for which a constant lookout is kept.

The crews of the vessels now manifest their discontent at the length of the voyage, and several of the sailors on the Santa Maria gather together in little groups and vent their dissatisfaction in loud complaints against Columbus.

THE MUTINY ON THE SANTA MARIA.

Upon the latter being informed of their mutinous action, he appears before them, soothing some, stimulating the pride and avarice of others, and threatening the more refractory with punishment should they attempt anything to impede the voyage, which had the effect of quelling the mutiny.

While Columbus and his pilot and several of the mariners are studying the map they discover Martin Alonzo Pinzon at the stern of his vessel pointing to the horizon, and behold him signal, "Land!" whereupon Columbus throws himself upon his knees to return thanks to God, but the supposed land turns out to be a cloud, to the great disappointment of all. The sun having set night now approaches.

COLUMBUS SEEING LAND.

While Columbus is standing on the deck intently gazing into the darkness he discovers in the distance a small moving light, which seems to dance up and down upon the water far away in front of the vessel. He calls Pedro Gutierrez' attention to it and then Rodrigo Sanchez, who confirm the discovery. Columbus considers this a most positive evidence of land.

The report of a gun fired on the Pinta now gives the joyful signal that land is seen, when Columbus and all the crew fall on their knees and join in a chorus of thanks.

Morning breaks upon the vessels when the land is plainly seen by all and the ships now come to anchor.

SCENE IV.

Columbus in the New World, October 12, 1492.

The ships having lain at anchor all night, morning finds the crews impatient to land upon the shores of the new-found territory. Many of the strange people inhabiting the island are seen arriving from all points and gathering upon the shore to watch the big ships, the like of which they had never seen before.

Columbus and some of his followers are now seen approaching the shore in small boats, the discoverer richly attired in scarlet, holding the royal standard of Spain, standing in the forward part of one of the boats,

THE LANDING OF COLUMBUS OCT. 12TH 1492

while Alonzo Pinzon and Vicente Yanez, his brother, each with banners of the enterprise, are seen in the other boats. As the boats approach the shore the Indians fly in dismay to the woods, and from their place of safety watch the landing of Columbus.

As soon as the boats ground upon the beach Columbus steps out upon the land and throws himself upon his knees, kissing the earth, and with tears in his eyes returns thanks to Heaven for the successful termination of his voyage of discovery.

His example is followed by all the others. Columbus then rises, draws forth his sword, while planting the royal standard in the ground, and assembling around him his captains and followers, with Rodrigo Escobedo, the notary, Rodrigo Sanchez and all the rest of those who have landed with him, takes solemn and formal possession of the new-found territory in the names of Ferdinand and Isabella of Spain.

TRIUMPHAL CHORUS OF SPANISH SOLDIERS AND SAILORS.

Salve, salve, la nostra bandiera,
Porta il bacio d'Iberico suol,
Nova gloria piu fulgida e altera
E serbata a ogni prode Spagnuol.

Behold ! our glorious flag, thrown to the breeze,
Breathes to the air a gentle kiss of Spain;
With each brave Spaniard who has dared the seas,
A great and brilliant glory will remain.

The crews, in ecstacies of delight, now crowd around the admiral with every manifestation of zeal, some embracing him, others kissing his hands and many begging his forgiveness for former doubts and complaints.

The Indians, ascertaining that no harm is intended them by the strangers, grow bolder and approach the Spaniards, frequently prostrating themselves in token of submission and friendship, until finally, coming closer, they gaze with wonder and awe upon the splendid dress and armor of the soldiers, examine the keen edges of the swords and curiously feel the beards on the faces of the sailors.

Columbus, pleased with their extreme gentleness, distributes presents among them of beads, bells and trinkets, which they receive eagerly, hanging the beads around their necks and seeming to take great delight in the tinkling of the bells.

In return for these presents the Spaniards are given parrots, cotton yarns and cakes of cassava bread. The Spaniards, noticing gold rings in the noses of the natives, point to them and exchange trinkets for them.

COLUMBUS TAKING POSSESSION OF THE NEW WORLD.

A grand chorus of triumph now takes place, at the conclusion of which Columbus administers the oath of allegiance to all his followers, and the Indians, appearing now from all parts, gather around the Spaniards in vast numbers until the whole scene becomes one of animated grandeur and is a true realistic reproduction of the memorable event just as it occurred on the morning of October 12, 1492.

CHORUS.

Alfine il sogno ardente s'é avverrato,   At last the golden dream its truth has shown—
Ecco la nova terra spunta già.   New worlds before us lie in beauty rare.
Stanna e questo giorno avventurato   This happy day, when centuries have flown,
Che immortale ai posteri sarà.   Will be remembered. Oh, the land is fair,—
A te gloria, O Colombo; il serto aurato   Upon thy brows, Columbus, placed by fame,
Sulla tua fronte ognora brillerà.   A golden crown will glorify thy name.

While Columbus and his followers are kneeling in profound meditation

A VISION OF PROGRESS AND CIVILIZATION

appears before his ecstatic eyes, revealing to him the wonderful results in invention, science and art which future generations will glorify as the result of his stupendous discovery.

Having now taken possession of the newly-discovered land in the name of the Castilian sovereigns, Columbus and his followers bid farewell to the natives and return to their caravels.

SCENE V.

Columbus' Triumphal Return to Barcelona, April, 1493.

CAST OF CHARACTERS IN THIS SCENE.

Christopher Columbus.
Ferdinand of Spain.
Ysabella of Spain.
Prince Juan, their Son.
The Marchonese de Moya.
Ambassadors of England, France, Venice, Genoa, Portugal, Naples, Germany and Scandinavia.
Magistrates of Barcelona.
Nobles, Courtiers, Knights, Soldiers, Hidalgoes, Standard Bearers, Royal Guards, Pages, Clergy, People, etc., etc.

The scene presented now is one of grandeur and magnificence, and represents the city of Barcelona on the day of Columbus' arrival. The return voyage of the great discoverer has been successfully accomplished, and, after landing at Palos, the little port he had first started from, he had proceeded to Barcelona to meet the king who had

THE TRIUMPHAL ENTRY OF COLUMBUS AT BARCELONA UPON HIS RETURN FROM THE DISCOVERY OF AMERICA

ordered a general holiday. Triumphal arches are erected in the streets which are filled by the populace, and church bells are ringing.

Soon heralds approach proclaiming the opening of the fete and the coming of the grand triumphal procession. Choruses of song fill the air welcoming the hero of the age. The music of grand military bands is heard in the distance. People rush to various places to get a view of the pageant, which soon makes its appearance.

The nobility and magistrates proceed to the city gates to welcome the great navigator.

TRIUMPHAL ENTRY OF COLUMBUS INTO BARCELONA.

Columbus and his followers, together with the Indians he brought with him from the New World, bring up the rear of this grand pageant,

COLUMBUS BEFORE FERDINAND & ISABELLA ON HIS RETURN FROM THE DISCOVERY OF AMERICA.

with the specimens of the plants, animals, gold and precious stones found in the new territory.

ENTRANCE OF COLUMBUS INTO BARCELONA. CHORUSES IN PROCESSION.

Queste son le damigelle,
Sorridenti alme gentil ;
Sono ricche e sono belle,
Sembran fiori d'almo April.

As welcome as the April flowers,
Here come the smiling ladies fair;
Full well they know their beauty's powers,
And for men's hearts they lay a snare.

Gli studenti sfilan lieti
Da perfetti baccelier
Studian legge, e son poeti
Colla mandola e bicchier.

Ha ! ha ! the jovial students pass,
Laughing, in careless fancy free;
They much prefer the lute and glass
To working hard for their degree.

O vessillo, di vittoria
Ci additasti tu il cammin ;
Sii tu guida a nova gloria,
Sii di Iberia alma e destin.

Victorious standard, flag of Spain,
In foremost ranks thou'lt ever be;
Glory and honor in thy train
Shall follow; all shall bow to thee.

L'andalusa innamorata
Passa a braccio al mattador ;
Di Siviglia e di Granata,
Viva, viva il toreador.

See, the dark-eyed Spanish maiden
To the matador is clinging;
Every glance with love is laden—
People loud his deeds are singing.

Quanta gioja e quanta festa
Qual tripudio in ogni cor ;
Col piacer gira la testa,
Freme l'alma a tal fulgor.

How much gladness, how much pleasure
Now is seen on every face;
Happiness, the soul's chief treasure,
Drives out grief and takes its place.

Questi son gli ambasciatori,
D'altre genti son campion—
Ecco Italia, e Francia, e Mori,
D'Inghilterra i gonfalon.

Standards proud from many a nation,
Britain, Italy and France,
All unite in exultation,
As triumphant they advance.

Sono i bimbi paffutelli
Delle scuole ;—Eccoli quà,
Sono vispi, sono belli
Vanto onor della città.

From the school the boys returning,
Bring our youth to us again;
With high hopes and valor burning,
They're the future men of Spain.

I soldati prodi e fieri
Forti in armi e lieti ognor ;
Son guidati dagli alfieri
I compioni del valor.

The brave defenders of our land,
Tho' bold in war, rejoice in peace;
Beneath their leader's stern command,
Their vigilance will never cease.

O stupor ! Ecco gli Indiani
Portan doni al nostro Re ;
O che volti oscuri e strani !
Son le donne belle, affé.

Oh ! sight most strange, with faces brown
The Indians come; their gifts most rare
For our great King will grace his crown—
Behold ! their women are most fair.

O Colombo, al tuo passaggio
Come vivo astro del ciel.
Freme l'aura e fulge il raggio
D'una glori senza vel.

Oh Columbus ! at your passing
All the air's with rapture thrilled,
And the stars, more brilliant flashing,
Makes the sky with radiance filled.

Salve, salve della Spagna
Re possente, Augusto Re.
Salve a te dolce Sovrana,
Alma pura, Salve a te.

Shout ! let people good and loyal,
Praise a Queen so true and tender,
Praise a King so truly royal,
He's the faith's sincere defender.

Salve, Genio immortale !
Nel cielo mai brilló piu viva stella,
Mai di gloria al fulgor piu ardente sale
L'inne festante che a noi era novella
Segna a cotesta eguale,.
Salve, O Colombo a te Genio immortale !

In heaven ne'er did shine such glory,
As thou bring'st to dull earth here.
Yes, thy name will live in story—
Future empires hold thee dear.
Columbus, hail ! to thee all homage pay.
In ages past, in future and to-day.

The procession now halts before the throne of Ferdinand and Isabella. Columbus steps forward, presenting the Indians and the ornaments, with all the other evidences of his discovery, and is most cordially received by the royal pair, who confer titles and honors upon him in return for his great achievements. All now kneel in praise while the grand national anthem is chanted, accompanied by the majestic organ of the church.

Columbus is now escorted by the sovereigns to the royal terrace and views the splendid festivities in his honor. The city now becomes brilliantly illuminated. The people appear with torches and the scene becomes one of animated gaiety.

A GRAND FINALE OF JOY.

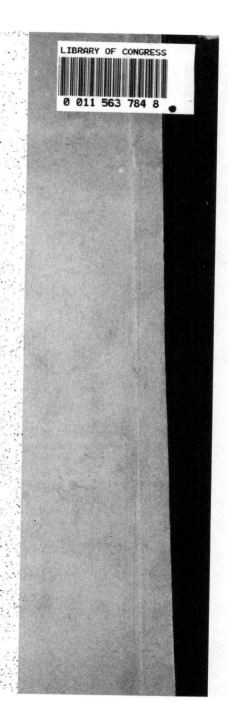

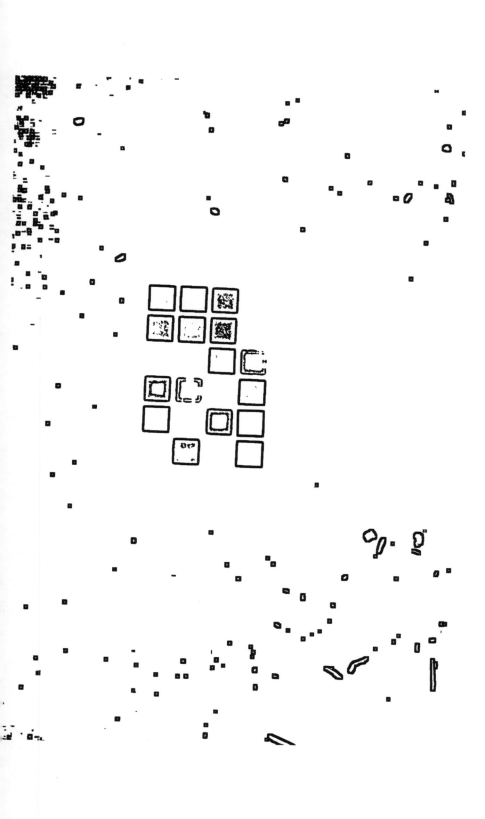

Lightning Source UK Ltd.
Milton Keynes UK
UKHW051000140521
383564UK00022B/270